When you get into
a tight place
and it seems
you can't go on...
   hold on
for that's just the place
   and the time
when the tide will turn.

Harriet Beecher Stowe

*The lowest ebb
is the turn of the tide.*

If there is no wind, row.

*He only never fails
who never attempts.*

Our greatest glory
is not in never failing,
but in rising up
everytime we fall.

                        Confucius

Out of your weakness shall come your strength.

The Bible

*The force of the waves
is in their persistence.*

Gila Guri

*Many strokes
though with a little axe,
hews down and fells
the hardest timbered oak.*

Shakespeare

Failure is the opportunity to begin again more intelligently.

Henry Ford

> The greater the obstacle
> the more the glory in
> overcoming it.
>
> — Confucius

*The door of success
swings
on the hinges of obstacles.*

*Nothing relieves
and ventilates the mind
like a resolution.*

                         John Burroughs

*Never take counsel
of your fears.*

Andrew Jackson

*It is characteristic
of wisdom
not to do
desperate things.*

Thoreau

*We are supposed
　　to forgive everyone;
<u>everyone</u> includes ourself.*

*Tough times never last,
tough people do.*

Robert Schuller

That which is within us
　　is stronger
than that which is without.

> The steps of faith fall
> on the seeming void
> and find the rock
> beneath.
>
> John Greenleaf Whittier

Faith is the force of life.

Tolstoy

*When you hoist
 the sail of faith
It is the wind,
 not the sail,
 that counts.*

*When anger arises
think of the consequences.*

> *Confucius*

The great remedy for anger is delay.

Seneca

Whatever may happen,
every kind of fortune
is to be overcome
by bearing it.

Virgil

This too shall pass away.

*In every adversity
there are the seeds of
an equal or greater opportunity.*

Clement Stone

*Oh, but man's reach
  should exceed his grasp,
or what is heaven for.*

Browning

*I steer my boat
with hope...
leaving fear astern.*

                Thomas Jefferson

*Courage in danger
is half the battle.*

Plautus

*It is better to light
a small candle
than to curse the darkness.*

Confucius

*The nearer the dawn
the darker the night.*

                     Longfellow

The only man
> who never makes mistakes
is the man
> who never does anything.

*Our doubts are traitors
and make us lose
the good we oft might win
by failing to attempt.*

Shakespeare

...in due season we shall reap if we do not lose heart.

The Bible

*Have patience —
everything is difficult
before it is easy.*

Saadi

This is a world of action,
and not for moping
and droning in.

> Dickens

*Let us then be up and doing
with a heart for any fate.
Still achieving,
still pursuing
learn to labor and to wait.*

       Longfellow

Press on. Nothing in the world can take the place of persistence.
Talent will not;
nothing is more common than unsuccessful men with talent...
Education alone will not;
the world is full of educated derelicts.
Persistence and determination alone are omnipotent.

Calvin Coolidge

*The human spirit is stronger than anything
    that can happen to it.*

When.....
   it seems you can't go on...
   hold on
   for that's just the place
   and the time
   when the tide will turn.